Mercy
Island

ISBN 978-0-9866909-2-1

©2011 by Ren Katherine Powell
Edited and designed by Elizabeth Adams
Cover photograph ©2011 by Marja-Leena Rathje, www.marja-leena-rathje.info

First Edition

Published by Phoenicia Publishing, Montreal
www.phoeniciapublishing.com

Mercy
Island

new and selected poems by

Ren Powell

PHOENICIA PUBLISHING
MONTREAL

Contents

|

A Poem for Loki

Knee-deep in the North Sea, Sigyn empties the bowl of venom. The earth shakes; the water trembles words.

Ever cold, ever rounder: rolled by the ebb, a cursive she grabs by the tail and hangs to dry. Not a fish, but a poem.

Red-Eared Slider

I

Suddenly, like rotting wood shooting out of the lake:
The photograph of Toby
straddling the cement tortoise.

It must have been taken with an Instamatic camera
because everyone had one in the 70s.

Odd, the details we remember clearly and those we don't.

It was somebody's birthday:
Rose Park, California.
I'd been there twice
     and I don't go many places twice.

I remember the huge snake
slide that wasn't quite slick enough
     it burned our thighs
          before spilling us into
               the sand pit with
               the tortoise.

I read once
     we only remember
          things if we retrace
the electrical connections in the brain often enough
to build a permanent bridge
from one image to the next.

I'm not sure that's true.

II

A deliberate woman
Grandma's home
was the sound of running water
    of terrycloth slippers
        on crushed pile carpet
    of bristled hair-curlers
        snagging
        a nylon scarf
    of chapped hands
        turning the pages
        of a Mitchner novel
    of ten past one on Saturday
        when the whole house is clean
        but smelling faintly
        of the grilled cheese sandwich
        she made—buttered on each
        side of each slice
        of bread, first—
        cut on the diagonal
        served with a pickle
        and a napkin,
        even though I was the only
        one eating

III

Elvis is dead.
Somebody found him in his bathroom,
his head by the toilet bowl probably,
said Grandma.

Toby whatcha doin'?
Mamma's in Hawaii with her bowling league.
We're sitting on the couch with Grandma,
watching the news.

> Toby must have climbed my dresser drawers.
> Lucky the whole thing didn't topple.
> Now he sits on the couch,
> his hands an incubator, a lean-to, a tomb:

Grandma's roots shine
like Christmas tinsel,

> Toby's petting
> my fish.

Elvis's big, pale face
wobbles in the footage,
singing *Blue Hawaii.*

IV

Through the car window I hear
my eyes sliding over the telephone wires:
        electric guitar.

The only music today:
Grandma's in a hospital bed, white
like a cement tortoise,
like powdered women in old paintings,

like rich women attended to by maids;
the angel Raphael is pulling long, black gloves
past Grandma's wrists.

        Toby and me shushed to the waiting room
        on account of Toby's big mouth,
        the waiting room with its aquarium of angel fish.

And Grandma's pulling herself in,
like a tortoise hiding in its own shell.

V

I was born again.
Then I was born again.
He said they found me in a crack
in a rock in the Valley of Fire.

Easter morning
I was a red-eared slider
Peace sign
painted on my shell.

I got a new name
driving through Utah,
obeying all the signs:
watching
for the "crazy escaped Indian"
called Falling Rock.

I was Love—loved
like a Susanna,
whispered to sleep by the elder's
soft, blubbering bong.

I was Love, loved
like the naked little angels of the temple
in Salt Lake City where Mamma said
they baptise the dead.

VI

The facts:

- Henhouse courtship is messy:
  Cloacal kisses.

- The turtle daddy drums
  the turtle mommy
  on the head with his claws
  to get her in the mood.

- Orgasm manifest in nature documentaries:
  Convulsing, muscular thighs of the lion.

- A high fever will bring on convulsions.

- A cold bath will bring down a fever.

- There is such a thing as dry drowning.

- Girl Scouts collect tadpoles in plastic cups
  then toss them onto the rocks.

VII

There were three guns in our Kentucky house. Or two guns and a rifle, to be exact. That one bruised my shoulder when Daddy had me shoot it in the backyard just so I'd know how to handle it. Just in case I ever needed it. In case I ever had the time to dig the bullets out of his sock drawer and remember how to load the damn thing, before I really needed it. He laughed.

One evening he called me outside to watch him shoot a groundhog or a badger or something big and rodent-like hanging around the chicken coop. Just for fun, he said. It was winter and he left it where it fell, in the tangled shrubs that covered the creek. The creek never really froze solid that winter and I saw the dogs coming back every so often. That spring the dogs raided the mice nests, and when the dogs' stomachs were full, they came into the yard with the squealing, blind mice caged in their jaws. And we couldn't do anything but wait for the dogs' appetites to return. And Mamma said that just meant there'd be fewer mice in the house come summer.

Once Daddy was sitting in the living room, showing me how to clean the pistol. Telling me how he wouldn't hesitate to kill anyone who tried get between him and Mamma—But it wasn't the shooting that got to me. Not really. Worse was the gigging he did in the summers. Mamma would press her hands together, saying it was good with something wild once in a while, and he'd leave the three-pronged spear leaning against the door outside near midnight, bringing the black trash bag, the big, plastic kind, into the kitchen, and leaving it to spasm on the floor.

VIII

Toby snapped the fryers' necks
Helping to butcher them

One by one by one
So proud

When we ate the first one
I was envious

It was like overcoming
A virginity

IX

I washed for dinner and hit
my temple on the corner of the cabinet—
                           streaks of yellow behind my eyes.

Toby lay, still
sleeping in his fever, and Daddy pulled
my head against his ribs,
all his fingers,
curled and tapping,
his shirt, wet and darkening.

X

The first time
a boy
wanted to kiss me

I made him do it
underwater.

That's when
I knew I was amphibious,

when it occurred to me:
Everything can be overcome;

we can wash ourselves
of all of it—
the facts, the fiction:

A child unconscious	*A child consciously*
under cold water	*held under cold water*
experiences laryngospasm,	*reaches the breaking point*
asphyxiates,	*after eighty-seven seconds,*
but the heart	*inhales*
keeps	*involuntarily,*
beating	*but the heart keeps beating.*
five	Ashes falling on water
full	float
minutes—	like rotting wood,

every instant bobbing in and out of view.

XI

Toby was born again.
Chirping in my ear:
Oh, baby, it's how mystics make their living:
Every moment brings somebody
the Apocalypse:

      Decisive neurofibrillary tangle,
      Front-end collision,
      Fever.

XII

Pets that bought the farm:
Jack Russell terrier puppy, kicked by a cow;
Red-eared slider turtle, poisoned by toxic paint;
Japanese fighting fish, pet to death—

    I wrapped the kitten in a baby blanket, in a cardboard box,
    her ribs still heaving when I called Daddy at work.
    And Daddy said, "Don't miss the school bus",
    And Daddy said, "I'll drive right home", he said he drove right home
    and took her to the vet who started her heart three times with
    electricity like they do to people on that TV show *Emergency*. I could
    just see her jerking on the metal table. Everybody in the room crying,
    beautifully.
    Music. Credits. Reruns.

XIII

All the facts:

- Henhouse courtship is messy:
  Cloacal kisses.

- The turtle daddy drums
  the turtle mommy
  on the head with his claws
  to get her in the mood.

- Orgasm manifest in nature documentaries:
  Convulsing, muscular thighs of the lion.

- When a new lion takes over the pride he kills all the young.

- A cold bath will bring down a fever.

- Leopards hang their prey from the tree branches.

- In my Bible's family tree, the dead have no names.

XIV

Having sucked at the roots
these thirteen years,
Toby is a cicada,
loud with knowledge
of everything buried,
and everything that trickles down:

And it's Toby who tells me
how long it really took Daddy
      to step out,
       to smoke one
whole cigarette

while Toby's lungs were filling
with a deepness previously unknown

spring

while Toby's elbows
while his heels, his head,
a porcelain, bathtub timpani—

The same time it had taken,
Daddy to write
the porcelain timpani   (with the weight of his hands
on Toby's head),
himself into the story—
There's so many ways to read   a story. This is Toby's
overture.

XV

Toby skitters across the pages of my books.
His incessantly buzzing electric billboards
revealing

    all things unnatural:

        Raphael teaches Tobias
        to murder the demon Asmodeus,
        by burning the heart
        of a fish.

    all things natural:

        Turtles survive winters
        under the ice by sucking
        water into their cloacal openings,
        and absorbing what oxygen they need.

    means and escape bright beneath my closed eyelids.

XVI

The photograph may still be there,
in the attic of Mamma's Vermont house
beside the lake.
>   (In a shoebox
>   full of the kind of photographs
>   people take when obliged:
>   Christmas mornings, new houses,
>   twins straddling a cement tortoise
>   at a birthday party)
She's still there. Her fingers turning yellow.
Measuring life by each
>   whole cigarette
and living with the nameless,
with the death that forced my leaving
and forced her to dig her heels into the ground, finally,
>   to dig for Daddy's bones,
>   to drag the murky lake
>   that sucks and spews our memories,
>   to discover what Toby has become
>   having sucked up the African sun,
>   and taken the body parts of the gods:
>   Taueret, Sekhmet, Sebek and
>   Lutenbi—the tongueless crocodile god,
>   presiding over fish.

XVII

There are
no permanent bridges,
So I carry a continent
on my back.

And every thirteenth or seventeenth step
the weight has forced me through the ice—

I overheard
a gym teacher telling his students
how Americans can't walk through a moor
without stumbling.

But he had no idea how close I'd been—
deliberate,

> at his heels.
> He'd never considered the back roads, river-
> beds of America:

> This far north, there are few poisonous species.
> Men here are all too

careless.

XVIII

Buoyant with lithium,
I am the lightest
of solid elements,
winged island,
pulling away
from the noise—

Once a cicada, having sucked at the roots seventeen years,
        louder than the traffic in Alanya,
        electric as Shinjuku,

having shot up,
my angel Raphael, my silent
crocodile sibling unnamed
is also pulling away, only now,
to sink
like a petrified relic,
anonymous, in a
copper bowl of
holy water.

Statute of Repose

That fall she woke among the blueberry
and heather tangles—after her limbs
had ripened and forced a protest from the womb—

Years from now he will excuse himself—
find comfort repeating his version: how she
approached him, naked, full of questions,
her green scent a curiosity.

as a frog in a well

I am chirping and supplicant as a frog in a well.
Formed as anguished as elegant as a frog in a well.

Two a.m. the dripping faucet sings in the shower
a dream as round and as resonant as a frog in a well.

Rumbling over the moor a tractor darkly pushing
through the fog as dissonant as a frog in a well.

A red beach ball bounces into the thoroughfare
as misguided an emigrant as a frog in a well.

Tourist wedged into the line of a mourning party
snapshot as candid as arrogant as a frog in a well.

The sidewalk prophet announces in capital letters
an apocalypse as irrelevant as a frog in a well.

Inner Space Qasidah

"I can see that nothing is solid, no matter how it appears."
from the "atomobile" script for Adventures Thru Inner Space, Disneyland, 1973

Tomorrowland has new attractions
though everything is still a shiny plastic

with sticky finger touch and mouth and hips
and handrails hot then cold through every shadow

That day I stood beside the ticket-taker
and watched the people in the plastic cars

as some climbed out and others took their places
the cars would spin but never stop or slow

Like luggage on a banded carousel
the people disappeared behind a wall

but reappeared inside a glass-like tube
that tapered into shrinking into snowflakes

Because is not a reason, but it is
just like *Just am* feels blue-woozy scared

my sister sat alone inside a car
a gust of air conditioning took her

The ticket-taker pointed to the tube
and winked *No one really shrinks, you know*

then Mickey Mouse led me to the exit
to see my sister's five-foot five all still there

It's okay, Chicken my sister pinched my nose
she'd seen the wrong-way through a microscope

an enormous eye was looking back at her
her every cell the spaces in between

II

It's not a long drive from Disneyland
to home but still we had to stop for gas

the attendant pulled the squeegee over the window
he smiled—my every atom jumped orbit

III

My sister's key ring had a rabbit's foot
my fourth-grade science teacher knew mitosis

I know the human body is too fluid
I hold these truths to be self-evident

Bakersfield

My hematite-edged days
scorched between cinderblock and thuja
the screen door and the iron rungs of the jungle gym

air conditioners hang from first story windows
dripping imploding stars
retracting irises on the sidewalk

I wear red canvas sneakers
tattered over the toes
a shorts overalls with metal clasps

that burn my skin
like cigarettes flung in gesture
like whispers

I drink blue Kool-Aid
I eat peanut butter on white bread
I stomach the bile of a strong man

the embankment is covered with sour fig
succulent lubricant for cardboard sledding
green everywhere flower blood insect

I push the door open and shiver blind
metallic musty settles over me
stale flour falling through a colander

the old apartment is newly
sprayed white floor to ceiling
a yellowing plastic covers the carpet

stained with cat piss
residual hate
like ugly maroon slippers

In the innermost room in the darkest
walk-in closet
I know the doorframe is notched

four foot one three eleven
a mercury barometer
my slow lift off

This was my point of departure
an airstrip stretching clear
to the highway.

The night's sky is bigger here than anywhere else
tomorrow peers through
to see where it's going

to wink at me
like a prairie dog in the corner of my eye
midday-horizon flashing *wet road*

This Buick is the archeologist
screening my loose thoughts
artifacts line the dashboard

bobbing heads of powdered milk
memorials to government surplus cheese
thin trippings of insects on the window screen

a nickel for every noontime
Stay outside!
I turn up the radio

roll the window down
let my fingers splay through
pass through black

numbing like ice
like a seeping curse
a sidewinder's poison

I dare a driver pull out
of the truck stop
hooker stashed

in the sleeper birth
lightheaded no headlights -
Go ahead—rip my arm clean off!

I say I stop each mile
folding each measure of asphalt
seven times

perfectly utilized interstate
winking beetles all in a line
discreet galaxies

At sunrise desert hairy scorpions
bury scurries in the loose sand
a raven gurgles the Indian death song

of lizard tails and artifacts
the Buick idles
as morning's easy tortoise

crosses the road
I follow over softening tar
negotiating a new language.

Coupling

To have his lower lip
between her teeth
was sometimes enough

    her cupped tongue
to birth turtle eggs
    nesting themselves

in his throat.
Nothing is
as ugly as hatchlings—

as raw, as needing.
A press of bones,
the intimacy of knuckles in the

caesura of vertebrae. The bird's eye
of the moment of obscurity:
the hurt before pain

hold, hold, hold
before the pecking,
membrane and shell.

The long fingers
of the rainmaker
    fisherman in the desert

pause
    left ventricle squeezing
the valve slaps.

Legs, arms, teeth—
everything: mouths
of lungfish

gasping
in the wet.
It's not pretty, not pretty.

Inheriting the Garden

We promised ourselves we'd plant posies
but all that time the bed lay barren.

It was summer when we moved from that place.
And the world seemed filled
with the bursting of dandelions.

The former tenants of this house understood seasons:
snowdrops, lemoinei, jackmanii—

But now, here, in late autumn
two monstrous roses press,
vulgar against the kitchen windowpane.

And too often at breakfast
I find myself holding my breath.

A Creature Bearing Fruit

early morning wet
musty from the dream that gathers itself—spent
tip-toeing in the dim light
and the baby flops like a slippery fish
from the easing grip of muscle

A Matter of Course

First I saw the kitten, tiny and red
then saw, in her movements, the cat.
Then the blue eye, larger than the gray one

the blind one
the deformity of the skull
the infection

But I saw it all too late: as I bent to pet her
carefully. And I did it in front of my son.

Knowing it was too late to change direction
knowing she would follow in a wide circle around us both

I saw beyond the instant we stood at the corner:
The truck that would come around and catch her under its wheels
We don't need death today, not today, not today.
And she would scurry off to die—

    and it happens like that
    she goes on her way, and at first
    you think she's all right.

    And, if the bladder happens to be empty
    she can even survive a half-ton of metal on her back
for an instant.

Denouement

He left a razor in the soap dish
    a slick poltergeist
    a festering splinter
    a red and white exit sign

The Falling Action

Newspapers are wedged in his mailbox like acorns in a squirrel's cheek.
I wear his missing autumn like a stole—fox, bullet hole—until Easter.

A Stranger Passing

I

She wakes, lifts
her head from the pillow
and the dreams fall, settling
into the weave

I'll make some toast
to sop the yolk
she moves to shake loose
the down woven into her hair

the feathers' barbs grip
at her roots *Tell me*
everything
you can remember

II

Her ankles turning on the cobblestones
a cold wind presses a ghost
into her cochlea, *Tommy!*
I remember fetching the eggs

the rough beige shell speckled with shit
warm in the palm like a stone
upright like a stone, *Tommy*

III

I'll bake 142 loaves of bread
I'll knead for 46 days
I'll grieve for none

She feeds the gulls all winter
they hover over her balcony
insistent and she has not slept
for 46 days

after 46 days feathers fall from the sky
weave themselves into her hair, her cotton shift
heavy, she pulls the hen from its nest
bloody from pairing

Spinster's Shroud

She has fashioned for herself
a gown
        of hollowed egg shells
and white thread.

She has taken from the clasp and string
her great-grandmother's pearls
and arranged the four hundred sixty eight
        fawn moonscapes
to hang in their stead.

An undergarment of ivy
        woven to lift the dry shells
from her naked collarbones
is interwoven with the wild orchids
that adorn the bodice.

The crinoline is formed of dried bundles
of bugleweed, saved from midsummer picking—
        eight times in youth
and twenty-seven times
        since.

She has trimmed the hem with holly.
A train of evergreen.

She saves for the last
        to tie the knot.

Breaking the thread with her teeth
sliding the needle into the cushion
leaving open the door
        to the coop.

II

.

A Poem For Seedlings

Fern is a wisp-green word wriggled loose of an earth run through with Brighid's red fingers pointing to her ever-redder fingers closing around an iron crystal—not a core, but a poem.

Mingo Oak

This braided rug formed
hills and hollows
the shadows

under her cracked feet
broken feathers of the cardinal
long purring snags

The movers will roll it up
secure it with tape
before they carry it on their shoulders

to the van that will take it
where it will not be recognized
but accepted as useful

The window sash was left gaping
and last night's rain evaporates
imperceptibly and grudgingly

like traces of skunk
like corroding pennies
DNA she abandoned on cupboard doors

riding spindles in my cells
The white paint on the windowsill
flaking molded crack in decorum

I look away casually and scratch deliberately
an act I refuse to acknowledge
green burrows under my fingernails

This key on this rope
on this hook near the door
is leashed anticipation

that her fingers wore
bare and acrid
And this garden

a half-gesture
the smooth-stiff coat of newborn
morning wet clings to a neigh

The broad touch of maple leaves
falls on my shoulders
russet coaxing

like a care package
like her onion skin
lain over a fairy-wren's map

I shout down the mountain shaft
past the mountain teeth
that took her husband first

then stole her lungs
with stealth
shining cut porous

fine dust scattered at the slap
of a boot on a braided rug
airborne with the snap

of a work shirt
pinned to a clothesline
with chapped hands

I moan a lament
into the mouth of the mountain
across the mouth of an empty beer bottle

this is the good she left me
bitter with the intimacy of cough
spittle gritty as coal

her lament as coarse
as the white-noise of a flayed deer
deep growl of the mountain claim.

I beat the dust from my jeans
and step backward
until West Virginia

folds and tucks
into itself
woven mausoleum

The flat earth strewn with char
black ant hills
tightfisted monuments

to the Mingo Oak that reached 148 feet
stood 584 years before the mountain
first winked

at the people who ground their faith
against inconstant walls of soot
who dumped mine soil at the foot

of their elder
the white oak lies dead
slag gold to pay the ferryman.

The collapsing mine took
everything but the dust
and this bruised martin

forced from ancient branches
feathers shimmer at dawn
like Water Strider rings in the half-light

the Purple Martin leads me to Rio
syncopates the wind with each stroke
come spring come spring

sambadrome batucada
nest of rattlesnakes
fire through a seam of coal.

Graduate Studies

I

Even the old, wild-born baboons
leave off masturbating their thin dicks
to groom the new mothers.

Even fenced into two naked acres of Texas
barren females can snatch
and hide an infant

until it turns to leather
and a juvenile grabs and flings
the corpse onto its back

to play pony—
For God's sake, says Stephen, my supervisor.
Don't anthropomorphize the animals.

(He reminds me
each behavior is coded for statistical purposes
and playing pony isn't one of them.)

Yellow males charge, but shy away at the last.
But females can carry a grudge and creep up
hours later, to bite a tail clean off.

(During estrus
their asses are a
gorgeous red.)

They stare at us
in our tower.
Stirring the dust at their haunches—

It's only the skeletal structure of their shoulder that
stops them from throwing feces at us
like the chimps do.

II

I face the wind
for most of the orientation
and never hear how many generations
of Japanese Macaques have been on the Dilly Ranch.

Monkey chow spills from the tailgate of the old Chevy
and the alpha male climbs up with us
sticking one of his arms into the bag.
Oblivious to me.
Or maybe not.

And maybe it isn't pity that leads me to coax
the toothy old female to needle the system.
I know that by taking food from my outstretched palm
she risks having her belly ripped open
by a higher-ranking monkey's incisors.

Each animal is tattooed
and it's hard work.
Stephen guides me
as I do number 168:

> My arm going numb from elbow to fingertip
> steering the fat instrument's watery momentum
> over her right flank.
> Manifesting tiny beads of blood
> like panning for gold.

III

In Houston, the rhesus monkeys
are kept in isolation, because they might be
infected with Monkey B.
A researcher in San Antonio was bitten
and died three days later.

Stephen walks down the hall, toward them.
But he tells me to wait where I am
in front of the Mandrill:
Play-doh masked
monkish as a vintage doll.

From this perspective
it's difficult to count the number of cages
or the number of sterile, linoleum squares
between Stephen and me—
and the Mandrill

which is mesmerisingly still.
Isn't breathing.

Is breathing.
And its eyes—his eyes, wet and open

The rhesus' chattering gathers weight
Spilling from cage
To cage
To cage

IV

(1992)

Stephen calls from California
'Just to say hello'
but I'm living with someone now.

Holding the phone up to his front door for a moment
Stephen then asks, *Do you hear it?*
It's the rioting.

We both laugh.
We thought he'd left that kind of thing behind.

Paso del Norte

for Lilia and the more than 370 others murdered and missing

We'd gone to take photographs, the seven of us tumbling
into the bus from El Paso to Juarez. Three guys in the back
drunk and rowdy, ready to prove their manhood
by taking in a girl-on-girl show.

We later heard how they'd paid their money
and found themselves
watching a girl fucking a donkey instead.

They were still drunk, but
reading the newspaper silently
on the way home that next day.
Their revulsion perhaps more authentic than ours.

The clean, indoor market was specifically
for those of us who didn't want to get dirty.
Everything was eggshell and blue.
It hadn't even been possible to haggle for the blanket;
the man had me pegged for a naive college girl.
At the time I thought I'd paid full price.

In the outdoor photographs
I'd wanted to create a feeling of detachment.
So taking inspiration from the director of Fiddler on the Roof
I'd cut a piece of pantyhose to filter the lens:

> my camera's shutter slicing
> through the dull eyes of the children
> who worked their noisy, cellophane-wrapped
> chewing gum into my fists, demanded a nickel

> slicing through the bundles of squatting women
> with their long, darkly-matted hair
> who shoved their toddlers with both hands
> in my direction.

I'd walked in the middle of the street
to avoid the barefooted figure draped in wet wool
who smelled like the devil's tongue my mother threw out
when it blossomed.

This is the result I'd been after:
these pictures of oily puddles
mirroring the brown smoke of the maquiladoras;
and these of the girls
the women who work there for three dollars a day
until they don't show up
but are found
     in the field called
     Paso del Norte's labyrinth
and then replaced.

See these faces, bloodlessly
blushing like those in tintypes?
Lilia, is this one yours? Is this?
Deftly antiquated at seventeen?

Your mother's foremother in death.
Dear child, did I shoot you
without permission on the day you were taken
on the day before your name made the papers?

And should I use this blanket
of eggshell and blue
to wrap the remains?

This isn't a documentary.
I was never really present.

Sight Seeing

monks in sneakers took the steps
four at a time while balancing teacups
on their noses and outstretched palms

and I remember you said
I wish I had a camera
and you framed them

with your fingers and thumbs
tilted your head to the side
squinting and clicking your tongue

will you remember this
you asked

Fear of Traveling

Because I've seen a donkey fly—
spin mid-air after our bus smacked it
in the right flank and flung it from its life

as we travelled in convoy
—on our way to Abu Simbel
where Ramses having been
dismantled, is pieced together
a facsimile of his parts

Because in Rhodes the transparent fish
bit our legs and every beautiful pebble
was once a jagged piece of glass

Because in Turkey my son
cooed at the kittens
sheltering from the midday
sun in a crumbling alcove
until we saw the sibling
skull, open-meated still

Because we learned too much
from the guides' rote compliments
from the meals thrust through swinging doors
prepared by the same anonymous hands that tuck
sheets around mattresses, slide
pillows into crisp cases and
press the bluest of eyes
Medusa in our palms.

A Request for Sound from a Televised Report from Afghanistan

I see her
a crouching shadow   in the footage from Herat
        swathed in embroidery

I see her curled there
in the palm of the Talib's hand
she is   cardamom and mint and whispers

Let me unfold   her tongue
where our common language celebrates quietly
slow and sure as honey

Let me run my fingers
sororal over henna-patterned
scars singing atrophied   notes

bitter as the fringed rue on the mountainside

I will give her the days
of my menarche and listen
to what she will tell of her own

I will learn when she speaks
of secrets that are not secrets
            how a girl moves and gestures

            how   a gesture grows
curling like yellow petals of the giant fennel
and guards her womb   opens her lungs

                                             lets her speak

let her tell me
she has woven herself

with lambs' wool
                                             with joy

into the palm of any man's hand

Girl-talk with the Poet from Ramallah

We're touring the holms now
from the deck of this little ferry:

She puts her hand on my hip
the heel of her hand on my hipbone
puncturing my social bubble.
She says they tortured her
fifteen year-old body
in front of her mother.

Her breath sweeps the left side of my face
leaning into me
her right hand on my hipbone
our breasts nearly touching.

Seven months in prison, that right hand
holding her mother's left hand.
Her mother giving nothing.

I have a daughter of my own now.
And later, after I've worked up the nerve
to ask, she answers:
Yes, my mother is still alive.

Her body supported by my hipbone—
by my suddenly widened stance.
But her voice above the sound of the wake.

Djinn

Tiger beetles scratch against flaking paint
                              against window slats
I stand on the outside and Atika stands
                inside
and we trap one
                buzzing

green against adobe
            jewel against skin

Atika's fingers are slim
She ties a strand of her hair to one of its legs
and lets it fly

Djinn she smiles, warns
        Don't let it land on your head
        You'll catch fire

This Djinn, she says *was an angel*
        flamingo hedgehog burrowing—
        resurrecting

We take it to the graveyard
Atika says to let it
eat   the bones
           with ginger and onions
the food of the flesh
pried layer by layer by
six agile legs

Blood squirms along
the inside of my thigh

It's the mark of the vanquished
          Atika says

She looks at me
hard,   smiles
before she unties her
shining, black hair

When We Met

It was October
I remember because that is the month
that goes into double digits
and the birches start shedding their leaves
and the slender prongs of the rake twang
like bluegrass music

It was Sunday
I remember because the wind
had been blowing in my ear all morning
and the clanging of the bells had scraped the canal raw
And the tender afternoon was loud with the deep
hum of your words

Your story was spices and metals I couldn't identify
Your story wandered like the veins on the back of your hand
when you pressed my forearm for emphasis
or help. Do you know I hardened to bear it?
—recast by the friction ridges of your fingertips
whorls that spin ever-outward?

III

A Poem for Lawrence

In the Sahara the word ravishing can be held like a musk globe in a man's hand and acquire a tenderness.

His cupped palm is a pale crucible. The ash offered up, not as a sacrifice, but as a poem.

that she has known

Her gestures made tender and fine by that she has known.
Certain nothing can crush the spine of that she has known.

An image of bone and breath beneath transient aquarelle
lain over oil over form over line of that she has known.

A sandstorm whips the body to remap an evolution.
It takes more than earth to realign all that she has known.

Weaving a braid from the girl the maid the woman.
Three fingers trace the serpentine of that she has known.

The slow extraction of sermons from a ribbon of gut
leaves an unadulterated lifeline to that she has known.

Closed Compartment

Kareem dictates a letter from prison: Dear
scratch that

                  Kareem writes a letter
from prison

                      Kareem scrawls a letter
         from prison
from the heart:
                 too many limbs to a room
                      putrid exhalations
                      broken pens
                      disjointed clauses de-
          composing from the heart

                 Kareem scrawls a letter
                 of sinews torn from bone
                 muscle drawn into the liver

There's no space for the heart's surge
in a closed compartment
of the tibia and the fibula
and he can no longer feel his heart's beating

I was right the first time.

Kareem dictates from prison:

pogo stick

Hopalong Cassidy hops until noon on the pogo stick.
He's getting nowhere no time soon on the pogo stick.

An innocent visit said the cow *no one will ever know*.
She left a pockmark on the moon with the pogo stick.

Just as the weatherman predicted: the trade wind blows.
Thirteen lemurs escape the monsoon on the pogo stick.

Two saddle-sore cowboys in dire need of transportation
will duel at dawn outside the saloon for the pogo stick.

There's an advert in the paper: an injured kangaroo
wants to trade his hot air balloon for the pogo stick.

Four girls, three boys, two mines and a pogo stick.
Evidence to present to the tribunal: a pogo stick.

Adjournment

M writes letters to his god
     his new bride shoved aside
as they pulled him into court
his new bride they   shoved
into as they shackled his feet
took his clothes

M writes letters

to his god his new bride
on scraps of tobacco paper
        of toilet paper
while they set up chairs each day
for each sudden postponement

     of his execution

M writes	he asks
his new bride	come to him
even twelve years later	kiss
his chaffed ankles his paper-	
thin skin with	love letters
scratched	
pale and flaking	for his god
his bride of faith	her bosom
natal comfort	

her sweat sticky   sweet
as honey   letters
on scraps with   shit and blood
the body's   ever-
               shedding

M writes letters to his god
his god a young woman a bride of two weeks
a deathbed specter   of twelve years
a bleeding promise   of renewal
keening his slow death   interrupted

A bride of two weeks   twelve years
                           now waiting
at the gate sitting   on the plane
next to him
suddenly   garlic and mint
                           withered
this   breathing mortal
intimate and strange

Losing My Religion

I joined the flat earth society
and at the first meeting they fed
me pancakes and sliced pepperoni
they asked me if I wanted to remain anonymous
if I wanted to lie on my back and make angels
in the corn fields

then we held pennies between our palms
we felt the cool of metal
we felt each dome of space
between the flat copper coin and palm
fill with the inexpressible

Arnold Refuses to Leave the Asylum While Insane

The corridors are hushed, a chemical lobotomy cold
creeping into the tent he's erected on the authority's lawn

"symptom-free insanity"   released
despite of because of   *non-correctible delusions*
regarding   *the justice of the authorities*

a prisoner of the official
state of mind

Arnold pitches his tent a dozen steps from the asylum
digs his pegs into the ground
like judgments   like diagnoses

Listening

She spoke for hours
She spoke for years
for forty minutes
serving mint tea
cardamom shortbread

You understand
could understand
Maybe you, she says
She hopes this time
You maybe will know

She speaks of the hours
Breath is not silent
She speaks of the minutes
and the hollow things
they make of a woman

She fills my teacup
gestures toward the bread
I am arbitrary
Indispensable
A cup and a saucer
rattling in a hand

On a Door to a Condemned Building

A green-black cunt in painted lines
     like a shallow rune pops in dusk's shadow
        the recoil of subjugation
and all the boys swagger west
looking for something easier
     edging around rival aerosol

IV

Aubade

1.

Intolerable
sharp light off frosted asphalt
Let the crow keep watch

2.

Uncertain as maids
greens hover over the birch—
Cherry blossoms blink

3.

The egret takes flight
fist against the morning's glare—
Then wide surrender

Mercy Island

You left this morning while I slept
the rowboat filled with peaches

like tender cheeks like swollen words
the fruit we'd picked throughout the week

The pier is slick under my feet
the pilings smell of sea and rust

The gouges are white where dock lines cut
through soft copper-treated wood

Along the path long blades of grass
slip beneath my calloused feet

The dog's coat is wet against my leg
and gritty-cold like salted cod

We breathe small clouds into the morning air
she shakes and freckles me with mud

She trots beside and circles me
as diligent as any lover

I find two peaches that you dropped
warm as living as pebbled beaches

Fur and sand between my teeth
then sweet my tongue our lives reversed

Already autumn stakes its claim
unclenching fists of purple heather

The willow grouse flies low *go back*
go back and feigns a broken wing

The sheep bells' clanging rip the day
from dawn with jagged little tugs

snagging sundew and cotton sedge
to make curry heather crows.

A month or two to stock the shed
then shear the ewes for winter's lambing

I plant the lilies when the waxwing
plucks the last of the rowan berries

I find someone to mind the place
in summer buy a boat and sail

Around the other hemisphere
I gather quince along the Congo

I look for you in the tops of teak trees
I hope you're with the manatees

Sea cows like hobbled sirens
sweet like shuttered windows

Just once I think I see your breath
escape the river and feel it flowing

Between around my fingers
a parrot chides *go back go back*

Immigrants

There are fish swimming just above my ceiling
under the feet of the tenants on the second floor
I can hear them swirling the water
with each thrust of a fin, with each
slap of a gill, I can guess they aren't big
probably the size of pennies
copper, green and orange
but making a lot of noise
And sometimes the tenants upstairs
clog in Appalachian fashion
and the fish get really pissed-off
and whisk up a buzz about it—to each other
but I can hear them.
They say, "*Jesus Christ,*
I can't believe I left the Amazon
for this."

Ghulah

She doesn't like to come on Saturdays.
There are too many children out with skateboards
and bicycles this time of year. She knows
she might be seen and doesn't like to take
unnecessary risks. And yet, again
today she feels compelled to take her trowel
and plastic bags and walk the quarter mile.

At noon she takes the shortcut through the grove
the early summer foliage and rain
are welcome guardians along her trek.
Within the shadowed square of moss-veiled stones
inside the cemetery's boundaries
she can relax. There are no funerals
today. Of course, she has been careful, checked
the newspaper, but they've made mistakes
before, and timing is important, is it
a matter of days, or years? With flowers, careful
observation is the key—there are
a few who never prune the roses, but
still visit faithfully (and more than once
she'd almost been caught)—

Two thousand two
a man who reached the age of ninety six
and now is resting peacefully beside
his wife. A reasonable span of time
for one this old (though it's different
for children). The holly bush has grown
to cover the name inscribed upon the stone:
Matteus Anders Voll.

The ground is soft
from rain, and she allows her knees to sink
into the mud between the graves of man and wife.
She dares the dead to rise, imagines them
pushing back against her angry weight.
And wonders, if she were to wake the dead
her dead—if places such as this were somehow
connected under earth's uncertain crust—
Could she forgive them now?

Working the trowel's
long edge first, she scrapes away, exposing roots
as convoluted as her nervous system.
Then, careful not to cut the woody tendrils
she digs the trowel's tip into the soil
deliberately, gently, prying loose
the holly bush's roots. She sets the trowel
aside, employs her fingers at the last
to rub the soil from the hair-like ends
and lift the plant into the plastic bag.

She heads home and never notices
the mud caked in her hair, or where the stones
have chipped the polish on her fingernails
or where the holly's thorns have bitten flesh on
her forearms and her hands and made her bleed.

On Karl Johan

Where the train station empties
at the top of the pedestrian street
a woman in an orange down jacket
sobs in the summer downpour

and a man with a black umbrella
pauses, then hurries on to the Bristol

where another woman sits waiting
in a deep leather chair
wet canvas shoes
stirring orange pekoe tea and thinking

about the woman neither of them will mention
(the path rain over her cheekbones
down her neck
under the shiny collar)—

He had found an excuse to
adjust something about the handle
of his briefcase, leaning against the railing
then squatting with a practiced look of purpose.

He had noticed her clean fingernails
watched the rain beat her lacquered hair

and thought to wait for her
to wait for her weight to shift

away or toward him
to provide him with a cue—

But she continues to stare
down Karl Johan

a slack shouldered,
stiff-spined stick puppet
street musician settled into
one wholly unambivalent chord.

He'd jerked
the weight of his briefcase
the handle into place
in his grasp, and
gone.

A Strange Woman

Too often she waits
too long and the doors close
while she picks at the splitting layers
of her fingernails, flexes her ankle to feel
the snap of a ligament jerk her back
into her body
too late.   This time

they take notice of her breathing
the children
      watch her shoulders rise
            her bones tent the fabric across her chest
the children
      swallow instinctively against the empathy rising
            like bile from an unfamiliar core
the man
      too familiar
            eyes darting to the wet canvas of her shoes
      You coming, or not?   She shifts her weight and her left
hip complains with a silent jab, her right knee bends   the doors slide
shut

Eventide

Winter has left and the bright pong
of seaweed moves in from the shore
and tangles itself in the heather

Black lichen is slick with evening
She climbs the smooth boulders
to watch the sea
unroll

Where once women waited
for the fishermen
Where once women waited
for the soldiers

she waits for the solitary tern
to spot a fish
and dive

A View from an Island

I am a Russian Doll
land within land

Sacred painting's
yellow ochre
my skirt
trimmed with lichen.

Something is lost
leaving the heather:

The craggy beauty
of an old woman's throat
the mellow man's joy—

Something is lost
to the morning's mackerel
as they slap Halleluiah
Halleluiah

Acknowledgements and notes:

When I confessed to Tor Obrestad that I wanted to write poetry he stared at me and asked, "Then why don't you?" It wasn't encouragement; it was his way of calling me out. I want to thank him for that, and then for taking the chance to translate my first book.

Some related trivia:

"A Poem for Loki" (original title "Saj 2"): Sigyn was married to the Norse god Loki, who was damned to spend eternity tied to a rock while a snake dripped poison in his eye. Sigyn spent eternity protecting him by holding a bowl to catch the poison.

"Red-eared Slider": There was a fad in the 1970s to paint on the shells of live turtles. Many died from toxic paints. A common sign in the mountains is, "Watch for Falling Rock". The story of Tobius retold in section XV is from the apocryphal book of *Tobit*. Taueret is the Egyptian goddess of fertility, birth and vengeance. Sekhmet is the Egyptian god of vengeance, wild animals and magic. Sobek is the Egyptian god of protection and fertility. He rose from the waters of chaos to create the world. Lithium is the lightest metal and the least dense solid element, and is used to treat mania—and to a lesser degree depression—in people with bipolar disorder.

"Spinster's Shroud": Young women traditionally gathered Bugleweed on St. Hans Day. It was believed that if a virgin put it under her pillow she would dream of the man she would marry.

"Paso del Norte": In 2005 the number of dead and missing women in Juaraz reached 370. The number is now estimated by human rights organizations to be over 450.

"Fear of Traveling": The Eye of Medusa is a talisman worn to protect one from evil thoughts and spells. They are commonly sold as souvenirs in Turkey.

"A Request for Sound from a Televised Report from Afghanistan": Giant Fennel has been traditionally used as a contraceptive and for respiratory ailments.

"that she has known": Under Taliban rule in the 1990s, Muhammad Yousef Asefi covered figurative paintings with layers of aquarelle to hide them.

"A Poem for Seedlings"(original title "Saj 1"): The mythical figure of Brigit associated with poetry, blacksmithing and flames.

"Closed Compartment": A closed compartment injury is internal damage common among torture victims. Swelling of nerves and arteries can cause muscles to die. Kareem is still in prison for something he wrote on a blog.

New poems first appeared the following journals: *Canopic Jar, Ghoti, Pemmican, Salt River Review, Weave, Yalobusha Review,* and *Black Robert Journal.*

The following poems are from *An Intimate Retribution,* Wigestrand forlag AS, 2009: "A Poem for Loki", "as a frog in a well", "Inner Space Qasidah", "Bakersfield", "Denouement", "The Falling Action", "A Poem for Seedlings", "Mingo Oak", "A Poem for Lawrence", "A Request for Sound from a Televised Report from Afghanistan", "Djinn", "When We Met", "that she has known", "Listening", "Losing my Religion", "Adjournment", "On a Door to a Condemned Building", "Closed Compartment", "pogo stick", "Arnold Refuses to Leave the Asylum While Insane", "Immigrants", "Ghulah", "Mercy Island".

The following poems are from *mixed states*, Wigestrand forlag AS, 2004: "Red-eared Slider", "A Matter of Course", "Inheriting the Garden", "Spinster's Shroud", "Graduate Studies", "Paso Del Norte", "Girl-Talk with the Poet from Ramallah", "On Karl Johan".

"A Creature Bearing Fruit" is from *Fairy Tales and Soil*, Wigestrand forlag AS, 1999.

PHOENICIA PUBLISHING is interested in words and images that illuminate culture, spirit, and the human experience. A particular focus is on writing and art about travel between cultures — whether literally, through lives of refugees, immigrants, and travelers, or more metaphorically and philosophically — with the goal of enlarging our understanding of one another through universal and particular experiences of change, displacement, disconnection, assimilation, sorrow, gratitude, longing and hope.

We are committed to the innovative use of the web and digital technology in all aspects of publishing and distribution, and to making high-quality works available that might not be viable for larger publishers. We work closely with our authors, and are pleased to be able to offer them a greater share of royalties than is normally possible.

Your support of this endeavor is greatly appreciated.

Phoenicia Publishing is based in Montreal. Our complete catalogue is online at www.phoeniciapublishing.com

www.ingramcontent.com/pod-product-compliance
Lightning Source LLC
LaVergne TN
LVHW051702080426
835511LV00017B/2685